DEZAREA DUCKETT

# THERE ARE NO PARAMETERS HERE

# THERE ARE NO PARAMETERS HERE

Copyright © 2023 by DEZAREA DUCKWORTH

All rights reserved. No part of this publication may be reproduced, distributed, or transmitted in any form or by any means, including photocopying, recording, or other electronic or mechanical methods, without the prior written permission of the publisher, except in the case of brief quotations embodied in critical reviews and certain other noncommercial uses permitted by copyright law.

Revolt Renaissance Publishing

# CONTENTS

|  | Page |
|---|---|
| **FORWARD** | 4 |
| **WELCOME LEADERS** | 5 |
| **PART 1** HUMANITY | 6 |
| **PART 2** MOTIVATORS | 26 |
| **PART 3** WINGS | 32 |
| **PART 4** ADVERSITY | 37 |

# FORWARD

I have been extremely impressed and motivated by Dezarea. The passion and enthusiasm that she has shown with leadership development can be infectious.

I've had to adapt to change throughout my 11-year NFL career, working with five different head coaches. Understanding different leadership styles is an experience that gives me an understanding of the subject Dezarea has embarked on in her writing.

Changing from a professional football player to a business owner, there are some similarities in leadership. You need a strong team to be successful. Every position or role is essential to achieving our goal.

Ray Mickens,

Owner of M2 Concepts

# WELCOME LEADERS

## EVOLVE AS A LEADER. GROW YOUR TEAM. GROW YOUR COMPANY.

Leaders face many challenges when managing the personality types of individuals from different cultures, backgrounds, and various ways of living. While aiding talent to become their best selves, leadership must also be cultivated.

Collectively, we will implement new strategies to grow our teams better. We will mitigate problems in real-time. We will focus on making the proper adjustments as we face challenges within our personal lives, and we will learn to distinguish members of our teams so that we celebrate each of them in ways they prefer, while making sure that we correctly handle the situations life will throw at everyone in their own individual ways.

# PART 1
# HUMANITY

Do you view your team members as human beings with emotions, or simply as replaceable employees at your company?

Our team members are human beings before they are anything else. Working with individuals as people and ensuring they are being treated as if they have emotions will determine the sun's brightness on good days and the flood plans when tides are high.

Humanity is seeing yourself in diversity.

People need grace and space to process their emotions while working.

**A Pisces created this module. Be ready to talk and potentially cry it out in our icebreaker sessions. LOL**

## ARE YOU INSPIRING YOUR TEAM TO BE GREAT ON AND OFF THE JOB?

Inspiration goes a long way, especially in leadership. Being inspired through adversity shows yourself and those around you that you are accountable.

A team is looking for a leader who leads by their actions. Your team's growth and individual trust are dependent on your guidance.

## PLEASE PROVIDE THREE WAYS YOU CAN INSPIRE YOUR TEAM IN WORK AND THREE WAYS YOU CAN INSPIRE YOUR TEAM IN LIFE BY YOUR ACTIONS.

# ARE YOU SETTING REALISTIC EXPECTATIONS WHILE INTRODUCING YOUR LEADERSHIP STYLE?

- **Tell your team about yourself.**
  Leaders set the tone. Be THE example by being open and transparent.

- **Empower team members to be confidently vocal.**
  Encourage your team to express who they are individually and collectively.

- **Set standards.**
  **Be the standard.**
  **Exceed the standards.**
  Inform your team on the basic expectations of their role, the consequences if tasks aren't met, and how to become a top performer.

- **Show your strategy.**
  Create visual strategies on how you plan on working with your team.

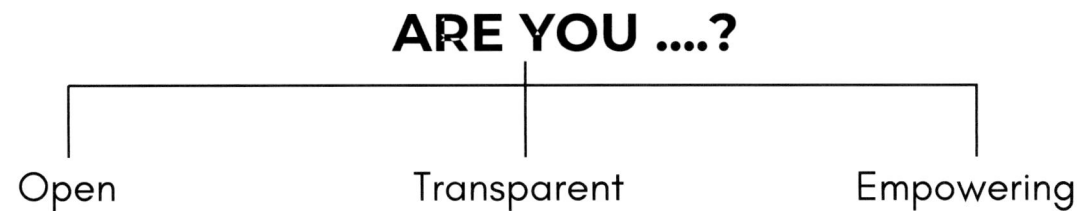

ARE YOU ....?

Open    Transparent    Empowering

## HOW ARE YOU ENCOURAGING OPENNESS, TRANSPARENCY, AND EMPOWERING YOUR TEAM?

# ICE BREAKERS

**1.** ASK INTENTIONAL QUESTIONS

**2.** CREATE UNIQUE GAMES

**3.** PROVIDE A SPACE FOR OPENNESS

**4.** CREATE WAYS TO RELATE TO NEW PEOPLE

## HOW DO YOU INTRODUCE YOURSELF?

_____

_____

_____

_____

_____

_____

_____

THERE ARE NO PARAMETERS HERE

## WHAT PEOPLE SKILLS DO YOU IMPLEMENT WHEN GETTING TO KNOW NEW TEAM MEMBERS?

## SEEING PEOPLE AS PEOPLE

Before personal issues arise (and they will), please let your team know that times won't always be great. There will be loss, grief, and sometimes even death. As problems surface, your team should feel assured that they aren't viewed as replaceable robots within the company. Instead, we will work with our teams to build, grow, and empower them.

## LIST FOUR WAYS YOU CAN SHOW YOUR TEAM YOU VALUE THEM

**1.**

**2.**

**3.**

**4.**

## YOU ARE AN ACTIVE WARRIOR FOR YOUR TEAM!

When a person is sick and worried about being penalized by the company, let them know they are people first and must take care of their personal needs before they can efficiently get a job done. If they don't have the time available to take off, as a leader, find ways to help them still get paid while taking care of themselves. Some people will call out of work frequently, but as a leader, it is your job to review all of your options to help those who genuinely need their sick days.

Make sure that your team knows that you have empathy and perspective.

## DECOMPRESSION SESSIONS

What are your triggers? What makes you upset? What do you do when it's time for you to take a break and breathe?

Decompression sessions are created so your team has time to process their emotions and life while working an 8-10 hour shift.

The proper space and grace will cultivate greatness.

How are your attitude and temperament when you aren't actively acknowledging your mental health and overall mood?

> ➤ Just as you deserve to be nice to yourself, your team members should also have healthy experiences in the workplace. Know their triggers and give them the necessary space to cope.

> ➤ Provide your team with the necessary space to exhale. People aren't robots and appreciate when leaders allow them room to vent.

> ➤ Set times throughout the day outside of breaks and lunchtimes meant for winding down and affirmation.

## DECOMPRESSION EXAMPLES

**1.** Setting aside time every day for your team to process any difficulties that come: work-related or not

**2.** Letting your team vent to you when they are frustrated with work-related issues

**3.** Allowing your team the space to communicate with each other without your supervision

# HUMANITY

**How often do you admit your mistakes and show your team that you are self-aware?**

_____
_____
_____

**How do you respond when team members point out your mistakes?**

_____
_____
_____

**How often do you try to look "perfect?"**

_____
_____
_____

**How often do you deflect?**

_____
_____
_____

**Are you actively being a human being?**

# THERE ARE NO PARAMETERS HERE

PART 1: HUMANITY

## WHAT MOTIVATES YOUR TEAM INDIVIDUALLY?

Get to know your team. Understand their personal goals within the company. Never pressure individuals to pursue something they aren't interested in; instead, ask follow-up questions based on what they are personally pursuing.

Intentional, direct conversation creates an understanding and connection between you and your team member regarding how you should coach them moving forward.

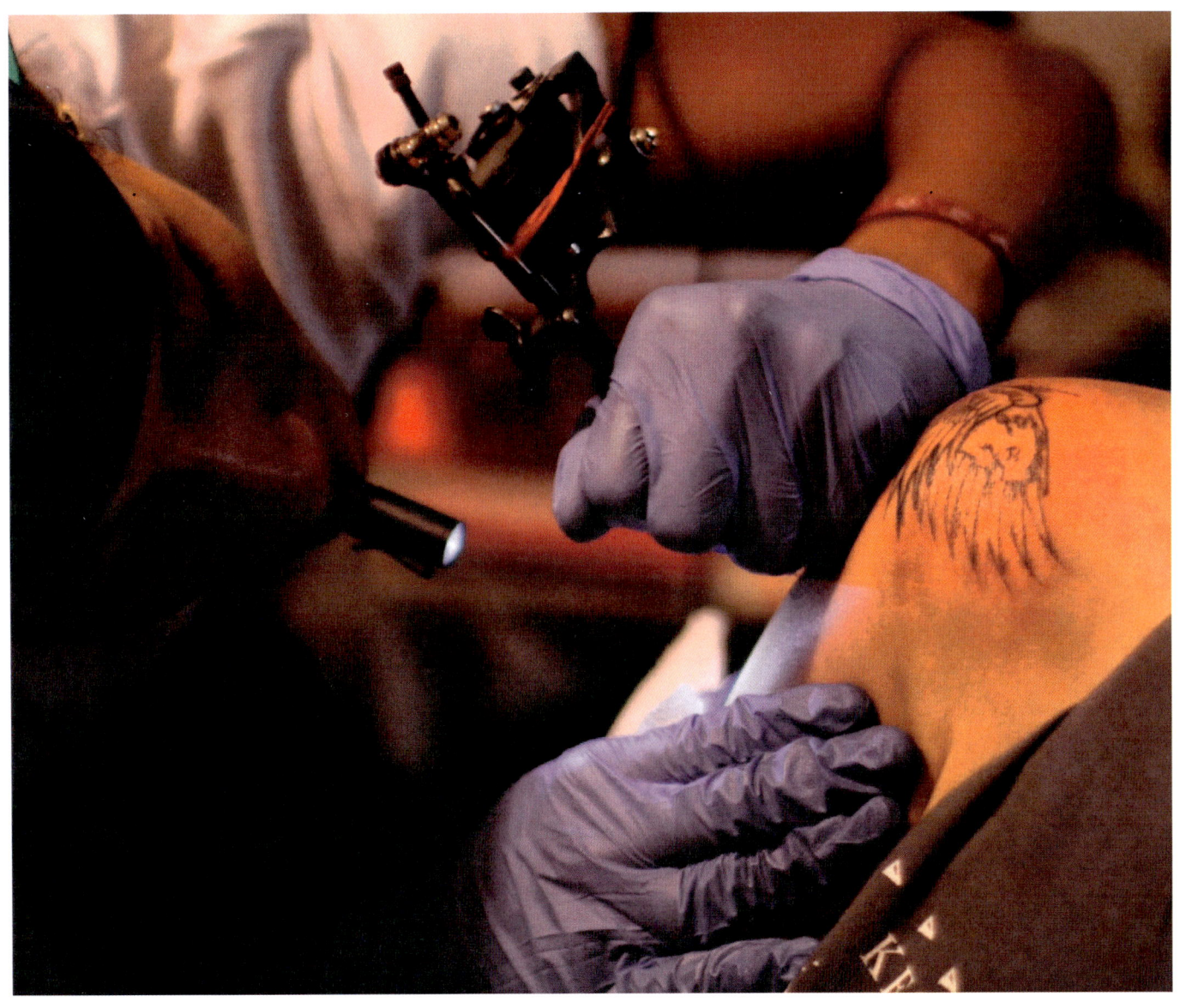

## TRANSPARENCY

Are you being self-aware?

## CREATE EFFECTIVE ENVIRONMENTS

Openness will create more efficient work from your team. Your team will feel more comfortable with you due to you being honest.

Sometimes we feel that being around superiors means we have to portray being a perfect person. Conversations are redirected, behaviors are persuaded, and most importantly, our working environment becomes anxious.

Create a space of comfort so stress and anxiety don't affect your team.

## CONFESSIONALS WITH YOUR TEAM BUILD CHEMISTRY AND CAMARADERIE

**How do you handle obstacles?**

_____

_____

_____

**What are some struggles you had before becoming a leader?**

_____

_____

_____

**What are the current struggles you have now as a leader?**

_____

_____

_____

**Are you willing to admit that you make mistakes?**

_____

_____

_____

## WHAT'S TEA?

When you were new at climbing your professional ladder, did you have a leader who showed you the ropes? Was there somebody in a position of leadership who walked you through the process of developing? Was somebody a call away? Did you have to learn everything you now know on your own?

## THE NEED TO KNOW

- ➤ Be ready to elaborate on the wins and losses that got you to your current position.
- ➤ Acknowledge the mistakes that you overcame.
- ➤ Understand the goals of the individuals before you and help them achieve.

**PROVIDE YOUR TEAM WITH INSIGHTS, CHARACTER TRAITS, AND PRODUCTIVITY THAT PUT YOU IN THE POSITION YOU ARE IN.**

## HONESTY
### HONESTLY, BE HONEST

It is critical that you are honest with your team about all of the information, whether good or bad, that you are informed of about the company.

Communication between you and your team ensures trust.

Be a person of your word, letting your team know about the good and bad news and not manipulating them with false hopes into staying or leaving the company. As a leader, you are dealing with people's livelihoods.

## ARE YOU A THERAPIST?

No, but frequently in leadership, you won't deal with ONLY work-related issues.

Be prepared to be open to real-life issues while setting the proper boundaries to distinguish professional relationships.

Listen to what your team members are going through outside of work when they present issues to you.

Most times, your opinion isn't necessary when a team member is venting to you. Still, a listening ear and a safe space will help guide the distressed individual to the self-reflection, conviction, and adjustments necessary.

When allowing team members to vent, listen so you can give them some solutions that promote their best selves when your voice is warranted.

## ADJUSTING TO CHANGE

➢ Make sure that you always have an open mind.

➢ Learn how to adapt to new personalities constantly. Value each of your subordinates by not putting them in a box and limiting them based on initial biases or assumptions.

➢ When a change happens in the company that isn't in their favor, provide empathy with team members.

# PART 2
# MOTIVATORS

# PART 2: MOTIVATORS

What are the key motivators for individuals on your team?

Know that everyone is not the same. Find each person's interests and your team's overall common goals and motivate from their unique perspectives.

## MOTIVATE THROUGH

- Competitions
- Challenges
- Bonding
- Inspiration

## GLORY DAYS
### LET IT SHINE!

One day throughout the week, take time to glorify the high performers of your team. Celebrating wins and achievements aid in not only showing high performers your appreciation for them, but small celebrations and affirmations will also amplify the lower-performing individuals on your team.

- Glory Days are opportunities for high performers to discuss how they achieved specific goals and overall team wins with the team.

- Create visuals for low performers that give them a roadmap of how they can achieve better.

## How do you celebrate yourself?

_____

_____

_____

_____

## Do you take yourself out?

_____

_____

_____

_____

## How do you affirm and treasure yourself?

_____

_____

_____

_____

## IF YOU AREN'T ACTIVELY CELEBRATING YOURSELF, THIS IS YOUR INVITATION TO START.

As a leader, it's essential to not only value yourself through actively patting yourself on the back and gifting yourself with the flowers you deserve, but you should also make it a practice to shower your team with praises.

How do you show yourself love?

_____

_____

_____

_____

_____

_____

_____

_____

_____

_____

## WRITE DOWN WAYS YOU WILL INCORPORATE YOUR FORM OF GLORY DAYS

## WHAT ARE YOUR FAVORITE WAYS TO ENGAGE IN COMPETITION?

➤ Watching competition

➤ Participating in competition

➤ Debating about competition

## POWER OF COMPETITION

One of the most televised media is sports competitions.

People love the rivalry, the banter, and the build-up sports bring. Sports have bridged racial gaps, started families, and given people reasons to fellowship on Sunday afternoons.

Implement friendly competitions to help team members achieve their highest level.

Provide rewards and incentives that are relevant to each team member. Refrain from incentivizing the prize you would be appreciative of; instead, seek to know what they would be grateful for and build reward systems around that.

## GAME

**1.** **Fun games help relax the brain.**

**2.** **Play games such as Jeopardy, Pictionary, and Family Feud.**

**3.** **Games can be implemented in an in-person or virtual setting.**

PART 3: WINGS

## SHADOWING THE GREATS

> ➤ Create a space where team members can work with each other without your hovering eyes.

> ➤ Encourage team members to have conversations without you present, as they are the players on the team. This strength in the team will be appreciated as they will see that you trust their decisions and ability to flourish outside of your initial direction.

> ➤ Let iron sharpen iron. When exposed to your team members' strengths, allow them to lead segments of given processes. Allow them to help other team members in their struggles.

## SHADOW SESSIONS

> ➤ Allow people interested in one day attaining the position you currently have to watch and observe what you do on a daily basis.

> ➤ Give team members who are interested opportunities to speak on what they would do if they were in your shoes as the team leader.

## MANY LEADERS HAVE PRIDE, EGO, AND ARROGANCE.

You, as a leader, have the opportunity to be thorough, transparent, and impactful without being disrespectful. Demonstrate these traits to the right, and you'll soon gain respect from your team.

- **Receive Advice**
- **Give Guidance**
- **Offer Help**

## ADVICE, GUIDANCE, HELP

As a leader, you don't work actively on the job that your team is doing. That's why you must be humble. You don't have all the answers. Therefore, good leaders are transparent enough to empower their team's voice by asking them questions.

PART 3: WINGS

Be vulnerable enough to say, "I don't know, let me circle back," and actually circle back. Give timelines on answers you don't have.

Value your team members enough to know their skill sets. Create space for them to lead the team based on their talents.

Let each team member thrive.

Ask each team member what they need from you to help them improve. Ask, "What can I do better?" "How can I make your experience better?"

There is power in allowing your team to work freely. Once you understand each individual on your team, you can then let them be free in who they are. The freedom found in these wings will ensure your team's best work.

➢ Why micromanage?

➢ There should be no boundaries on how work gets completed. Allow team members to get work done in ways that are conducive to them.

➢ Some people work good over time, some people need the pressure of working last minute. As long as the job gets done proficiently, that's all that matters.

## DO YOU PEOPLE-WATCH OR WORK-WATCH?

How does it feel to you when someone is looking over your shoulders? Are you as effective as you would be if you were given the proper space to breathe?

How do you hold your team accountable when their work is inconsistent? How are you improving your team's work?

Observing and working with your subordinates as equals are essential to your team's growth. Bounce ideas off of each other, ask and continually redefine the vision, and be supportive and inviting, respecting your subordinate's input.

# PART 4
# ADVERSITY

How do you work through adversity with yourself and your team?

Understand that everyone is not the same. Some people will not change, and the job is not a good fit.

So what are the next steps, and how do we deal with those stubborn employees?

**ARE YOU STRUGGLING WITH YOUR WORK RELATIONSHIPS WITH YOUR SUBORDINATES OR PEERS?**

## IMPROPER PLACEMENT

Often times we wonder why specific relationships don't work. In most cases, rocky work relationships are made more complicated than they should be.

A team member needing to be repositioned to a role that better fits their personality and working style could be a simple solution to the disconnect.

PART 4: ADVERSITY

# PERSONALITY ASSESSMENTS

While in leadership, it is essential to understand your personnel. There are a ton of personality questionnaires out there, but finding the one that best fits you and your leadership style would be the best option.

# WHY SHOULD YOU INCORPORATE PERSONALITY QUESTIONNAIRE?

Everyone is different. There is not one person that acts exactly like another individual.

## HOW TO WORK WITH DIVERSITY?
### ADVERSITY IN DIVERSITY

While working in diverse settings, you will have many differences in personalities, backgrounds, lifestyles, and cultures. Learning how to navigate those differences healthily will elevate your leadership skills.

Let's not be ignorant of the fact that our world is evolving. Many companies are hiring more diverse employees—from religion to race to sexuality. Whether you agree or disagree with the looks or preferences of team members, know that everyone on your team will not have the same beliefs as you.

As a leader, how you decide to collaborate, plan, and commingle throughout your team's unique structure will positively or negatively affect your collective unit and overall team strength and effectiveness.

## EXPOSE YOUR BIASES.

Whether aware or unaware, we all have biases. It is essential to work towards knowing what your personal preferences are so that you learn how you negatively impact your team's structure.

We, as leaders, are not being held accountable in our positions from the perspective of how we treat our subordinates most of the time. Therefore, as a leader, it is vital that you hold yourself accountable and be self-aware. This personal conviction and growth aid your effectiveness amongst diverse people.

### THE BASIS OF BIASES?

As humans, we all have them. Biases can stem from our personal and chosen families, friends, environments, TV, music, lifestyles, education, and lack of education.

PART 4: ADVERSITY

## QUESTIONS A LEADER SHOULD CONTINUALLY ASK THEMSELVES

1. Am I exposing my personal biases?

2. Do I flinch when I encounter someone/something against or unknown to my personal beliefs?

3. Am I opinionated when my opinion is not asked?

4. Do I welcome my team to confront me when I am displaying biases?

## HOW CAN LEADERS PRODUCTIVELY EXPOSE THEIR BIASES?

➢ Be honest with your team about who you are and where you came from so that people can know whom they are dealing with.

➢ Opening up to your team about your experiences in life and asking intentional questions so you can grow into a more empathetic person amongst your team.

➢ Placing yourself in environments that are contrary to your native language (tastebuds/likes) and culture help excel in world perspective and your overall career.

## ARE YOU CONTROLLING YOUR REACTIONS AND FACIAL EXPRESSIONS WHEN INTERACTING WITH OTHERS?

- Are you quick to listen and slow to react?
- Are you working to understand how your actions affect those around you?
- Are you using discernment before making a potentially reckless comment?

**Practicing emotional intelligence will make you a more extraordinary leader.**

## DO YOU FEEL YOUR OPINION SHOULD BE STATED NO MATTER WHAT?

We all are entitled to our opinion and have a right to feel every emotion we feel. It is in our human nature. However, what we do before feeling an emotion is a crucial action worthy of thought and reason. Opinions are very valid, but opinions should only be voiced when necessary.

While in leadership, you will often be asked to voice your opinion. Because of this power structure, many leaders think it necessary to express opinions when they aren't requested. Many personal opinions are rooted in our biases generated from our singular perspective of life. Therefore, be careful of giving unwanted 'gifts' and undesired 'help.' If someone wants to know your opinion, they will ask.

## EDUCATE YOURSELF SO YOU CAN ADEQUATELY FACE BIASES.

Constantly educating ourselves will not only assist with improving leadership quality, but it will also help provide more significant, more fluid perspectives on life and opinion. Let's challenge ourselves to be more open-minded.

Be willing to learn about a person's culture, selection of art, history, family structure, and entertainment without your interpretation. While learning your teams, be sensitive and open to engage and ask questions when necessary.

Constantly provide spaces for your team to tell and interpret their own stories.

## REMEMBER: YOU'VE GOT THIS, LEADERS!

There are many benefits to gain from expanding your leadership style. These practices should be dissected and implemented in ways that fit the mold of your leadership.

People work harder for people who have an emotional connection with them. Empathy felt reflects a sense of security. Knowing and feeling leadership has the back of subordinates helps ensure excellence on the job.

Finally, allow this training to help transform your team into emotionally-secured, power-working machines!

Made in the USA
Coppell, TX
14 November 2024

40082938R00026